THE WORLD'S STUPIDEST SIGNS

The majority of these signs were spotted by the Publisher. However, we should also like to thank readers of our previously published *Please Take Advantage of the Chambermaid and other Silly Signs*, who sent in their stupid signs to us. We should also like to acknowledge the *New Scientist* magazine's Feedback page, where some of the signs included in this book have appeared. If you have any signs you would like to send to us for a future collection, please e-mail them to **jokes@michaelomarabooks.com**

THE WORLD'S STUPIDEST SIGNS

Michael O'Mara Humour

First published in Great Britain in 2000 by
Michael O'Mara Books Limited
9 Lion Yard
Tremadoc Road
London SW4 7NQ

A CIP catalogue record for this book is available from
the British Library

ISBN 1-85479-555-4

9 10

Designed and typeset by Design 23, London
Edited by Bryony Evens
Printed and bound in Great Britain by
Cox & Wyman, Reading, Berks

www.mombooks.com

WEARING THIS GARMENT DOES NOT ENABLE YOU TO FLY

On a child's Superman costume

ICE CREAM TOILETS

On a campsite

WE DO NOT TEAR YOUR CLOTHING WITH MACHINERY. WE DO IT CAREFULLY BY HAND.

In a dry cleaner's

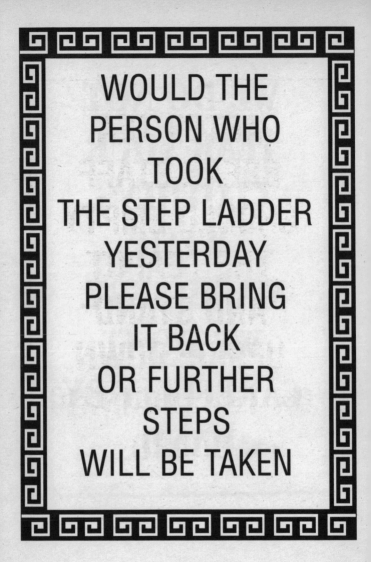

WOULD THE
PERSON WHO
TOOK
THE STEP LADDER
YESTERDAY
PLEASE BRING
IT BACK
OR FURTHER
STEPS
WILL BE TAKEN

In a factory

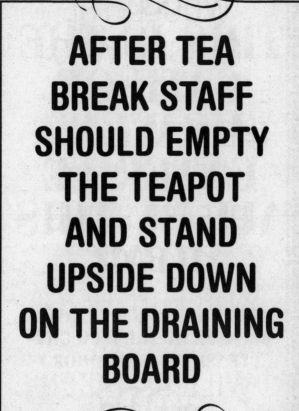

**AFTER TEA
BREAK STAFF
SHOULD EMPTY
THE TEAPOT
AND STAND
UPSIDE DOWN
ON THE DRAINING
BOARD**

In an office

THIS IS THE GATE OF HEAVEN. ENTER YE ALL BY THIS DOOR.

(THIS DOOR IS KEPT LOCKED BECAUSE OF THE DRAUGHT– PLEASE USE SIDE DOOR.)

On a church door

CAUTION: AUTOMATIC DOOR PUSH TO OPERATE

On the entrance door
to an office building

THURSDAY NIGHT POTLUCK SUPPER PRAYERS AND MEDICATION TO FOLLOW

Notice in a parish magazine

NO PURCHASE NECESSARY

DETAILS INSIDE

On several different snack wrappers

Mothers, Please Wash Your Hans Before Eating

English sign in a German café

THE TOWN HALL IS CLOSED UNTIL OPENING. IT WILL REMAIN CLOSED AFTER BEING OPENED. OPEN TOMORROW

Sign outside a new town hall which was to be opened by the Prince of Wales

SLOW CATTLE CROSSING NO OVERTAKING FOR THE NEXT 100 YRS

Seen at the side of a Sussex road

ONE HOUR PHOTOS READY IN 20 MINUTES

Outside a shop in Brixton, London

WARNING: HIGH IN SODIUM

On a container of salt

SAFETY FIRST PLEASE PUT ON YOUR SEAT BELT PREPARE FOR ACCIDENT

Sign in a Japanese taxi

NOT TO BE REMOVED FROM CREWE STATION

On a luggage trolley at Singapore airport

SWIMMING POOL SUGGESTIONS OPEN 24 HOURS LIFEGUARD ON DUTY 8AM TO 8PM DROWNING ABSOLUTELY PROHIBITED

Sign at a resort in the Philippines

WE CAN REPAIR ANYTHING.

**(PLEASE KNOCK HARD
ON THE DOOR –
THE BELL
DOESN'T WORK)**

Sign on a repair shop door

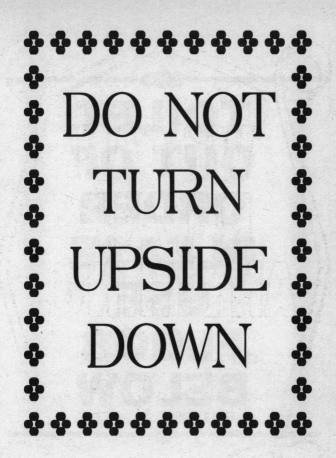

DO NOT TURN UPSIDE DOWN

**Printed on the BOTTOM of a
tiramisu dessert box**

TOILET OUT OF ORDER PLEASE USE FLOOR BELOW

In a toilet in a London office block

OPEN SEVEN DAYS A WEEK

(EXCEPT MONDAYS)

Sign at a New York restaurant

WHEN YOU CAN'T SEE THIS SIGN, THE RIVER IS UNDER WATER

Sign in a country lane

WANTED: EJECTION SEAT TESTER INVOLVES A SMALL AMOUNT OF TRAVELLING

Job advert in an employment agency

PLEASE DO NOT LEAN ON THE WIDOW

On a cruise ship

IN MEMORIAM

THIS TREE IS
A SYMBOL OF
OUR MUM.
PEACEFUL,
STRONG AND
SHELTERING
FROM HER
CHILDREN.

Plaque in a Midlands arboretum

WANTED

UNMARRIED

GIRLS

TO PICK FRESH

FRUIT

AND PRODUCE

AT NIGHT

On a farm

NO
CHILDREN
ALLOWED

In an American maternity ward

FOR INDOOR OR OUTDOOR USE ONLY

On a string of Chinese-made
Christmas lights

SLICED HAM WITH VEGETARIAN CHEDDAR

Pre-packed croissant label

SMARTS IS THE MOST EXCLUSIVE DISCO IN TOWN EVERYONE WELCOME

Outside a disco

MIXING BOWL
SET DESIGNED
TO PLEASE A
COOK
WITH ROUND
BOTTOM
FOR EFFICIENT
BEATING

Sign in kitchen shop

Sign warning of quicksand

A BEAN SUPPER WILL BE HELD ON TUESDAY EVENING IN THE CHURCH HALL. MUSIC WILL FOLLOW.

Sign in a church

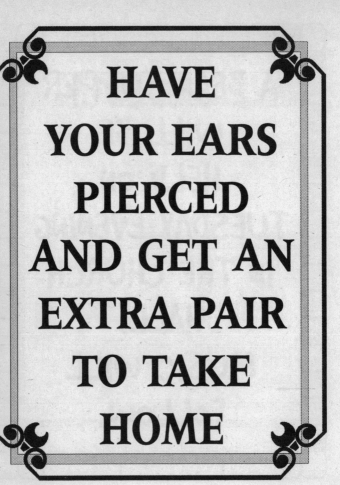

HAVE YOUR EARS PIERCED AND GET AN EXTRA PAIR TO TAKE HOME

In a jewellery shop

WE UNBLOCK YOUR CONSTIPATION WITH OUR FINGERS

Ad for an American reflexology centre

DUE TO INCREASING PROBLEMS WITH LITTER LOUTS AND VANDALS WE MUST ASK ANYONE WITH RELATIVES BURIED IN THE GRAVEYARD TO DO THEIR BEST TO KEEP THEM IN ORDER

Notice sent to residents of a Wiltshire parish

ELEPHANTS PLEASE STAY IN YOUR CAR

In a safari park

WARNING: CONTAINS NUTS

On a packet of supermarket own brand peanuts

INSTRUCTIONS:
OPEN PACKET, EAT NUTS

On an airline packet of peanuts

TEAR OPEN.
UNFOLD.
USE.

On a fast food outlet handy wipe

DO NOT ATTEMPT TO STOP CHAIN WITH YOUR HANDS

On a Swedish chainsaw

GOOD APPEARANCE PLEASE NO WATERMELON PLEASE

Sign in a Beijing hotel lobby

BARGAIN BASEMENT UPSTAIRS

Sign in a London department store

SALE OF LOST AND UNCLAIMED PROPERTY

UMBRELLAS BY THE THOUSAND, HANDBAGS, BRIEFCASES, OVERCOATS, ABANDONED CHILDREN

Advert from lost property auction guide

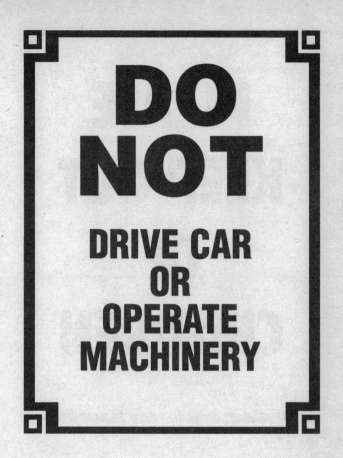

DO NOT

DRIVE CAR
OR
OPERATE
MACHINERY

On a bottle of children's cough medicine

PLEASE KEEP OUT OF CHILDREN

On a Korean kitchen knife

WE EXCHANGE ANYTHING

BICYCLES, WASHING MACHINES ETC WHY NOT BRING YOUR WIFE ALONG AND GET A WONDERFUL BARGAIN?

Outside a second-hand shop

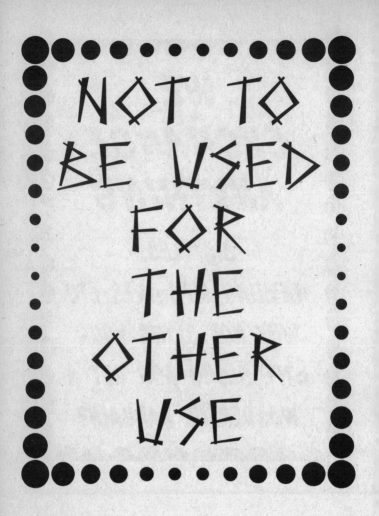

NOT TO BE USED FOR THE OTHER USE

On a Japanese food processor

HORSE MANURE

50p PER PRE-PACKED BAG

20p DO-IT-YOURSELF

Outside a farm

WARNING:
MAY CAUSE
DROWSINESS

On a packet of sleeping tablets

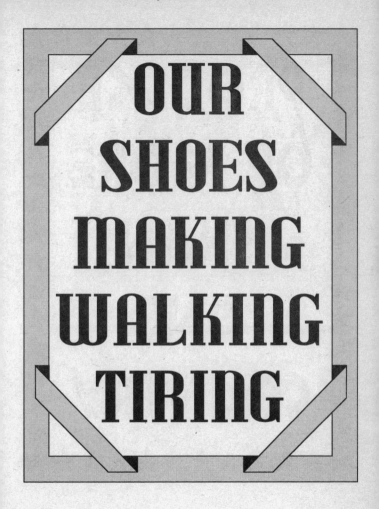

Advert for a Jakarta shoe company

PRODUCE OF MORE THAN ONE COUNTRY

On a SINGLE pre-packaged vanilla pod in most supermarkets!

DANGER!
PUBLIC MUST NOTE, TO KILL BABIES, INSERT THEM HEAD INTO BAG. CAREFULLY! THANK YOU

From the plastic cover of a child's surfboard

AUTOMATIC WASHING MACHINES

PLEASE REMOVE ALL YOUR CLOTHES WHEN THE LIGHT GOES OUT

Sign in a launderette

SUITABLE FOR VEGETARIANS

On a bottle of supermarket mineral water

THIS DOOR IS NOT TO BE USED AS AN EXIT OR AN ENTRANCE

Sign on door at a New York post office

NO
TRESPASSING
WITHOUT
PERMISSION

Sign on church property

PRODUCT WILL BE HOT AFTER HEATING

On pre-packaged bread pudding

FOR SALE CARAVAN'S EGGS

By a Derbyshire roadside

IF YOU CANNOT READ THIS, THIS LEAFLET WILL TELL YOU HOW TO GET LESSONS

On a leaflet

FITS ONE HEAD

On a shower cap provided by a hotel

SERVING SUGGESTION: DEFROST

On a range of frozen dinners

OUT TO
LUNCH
IF NOT
BACK BY FIVE,
OUT FOR
DINNER ALSO

Outside a photographer's studio

THE FARMER
ALLOWS
WALKERS TO
CROSS
THE FIELD FOR
FREE,
BUT THE
BULL
CHARGES

Notice in a field

Notice in health food shop window

DO NOT IRON CLOTHES ON BODY

On packaging for a steam iron

FOR ANYONE WHO HAS CHILDREN AND DOESN'T KNOW IT, THERE IS A CRECHE ON THE FIRST FLOOR

Sign at a conference

DIRECTIONS: USE LIKE REGULAR SOAP

On a bar of soap

SAME DAY

DRY CLEANING

ALL

GARMENTS

READY IN

48 HOURS

In the window of a dry cleaner's

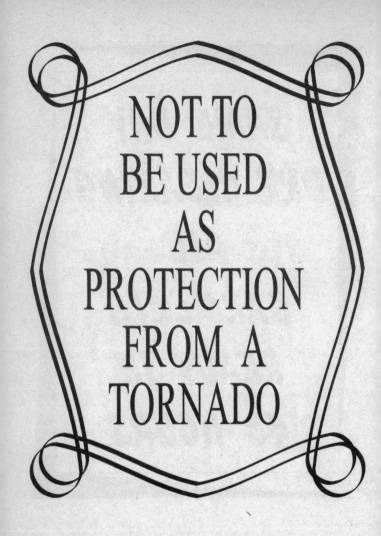

NOT TO
BE USED
AS
PROTECTION
FROM A
TORNADO

On a blanket from Taiwan

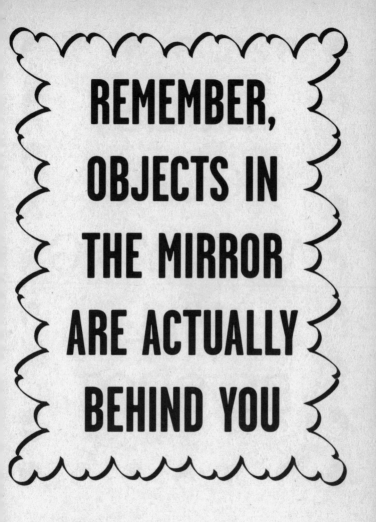

REMEMBER, OBJECTS IN THE MIRROR ARE ACTUALLY BEHIND YOU

On a helmet mounted mirror used by US cyclists

DOGS FOUND WORRYING WILL BE SHOT

Sign on a farm gate

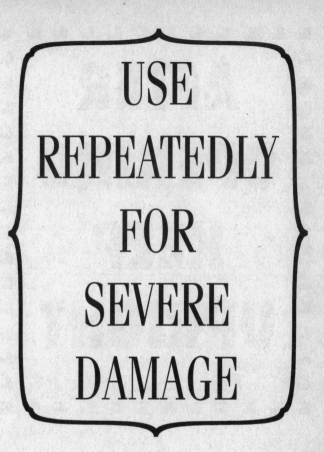

USE REPEATEDLY FOR SEVERE DAMAGE

On a Taiwanese shampoo

AFTER OPENING KEEP UPRIGHT

On the bottle-top of a flavoured milk drink

Low
SELF ESTEEM
SUPPORT GROUP
MEETS THURSDAY
AT 7PM

PLEASE USE
THE BACK DOOR

Sign in church hall

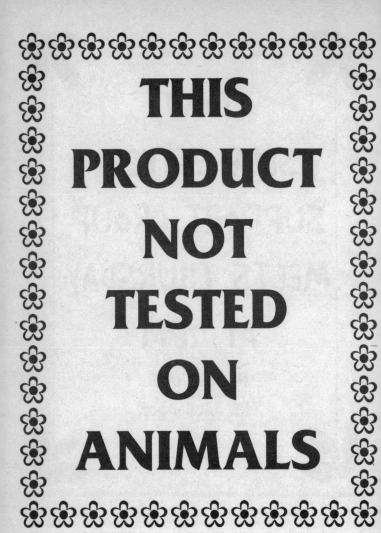

THIS PRODUCT NOT TESTED ON ANIMALS

On a New Zealand insect spray

PLEASE
DO NOT
FEED THE
ELEPHANTS

IF YOU HAVE
ANY PEANUTS
OR BUNS
GIVE THEM TO
THE KEEPER
ON DUTY

At the zoo

TO AVOID CONDENSATION FORMING, ALLOW THE BOXES TO WARM UP TO ROOM TEMPERATURE BEFORE OPENING

In a US guide to setting up a new computer found INSIDE the box

NO WALKING, SITTING OR PLAYING ON THE GRASS IN THIS PLEASURE PARK

Notice in a London park

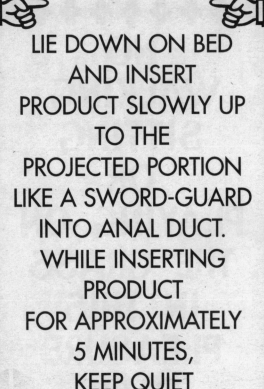

LIE DOWN ON BED
AND INSERT
PRODUCT SLOWLY UP
TO THE
PROJECTED PORTION
LIKE A SWORD-GUARD
INTO ANAL DUCT.
WHILE INSERTING
PRODUCT
FOR APPROXIMATELY
5 MINUTES,
KEEP QUIET

**On a Japanese product used to
relieve painful haemorrhoids**

WE REPAIR WHAT YOUR HUSBAND FIXED

Sign on a repair shop door

OPEN OTHER END

**In some countries,
on the BOTTOM of cola bottles**

WHY NOT TRY TOSSING OVER YOUR FAVOURITE BREAKFAST CEREAL?

On a packet of raisins

FOR
SALE
BUY
OWNER

Private sale board outside a house

In a Mexico City hotel

EAT HERE GET GAS FREE

Outside an American service station

WARNING

REMOVE CHILD BEFORE FOLDING

On a pushchair

YOU HAVE
NO REASON
TO TRY
OUR
BEST
RESTAURANT

**Sign in an Indonesian
hotel restaurant**

MAKE FACIAL CUT

Sign in Japanese beauty parlour

VOLUME ON.
SQUELCH.
PLEASE DIAL
TO SHUT
WHENEVER
YOU WANT TO

Sign in a Tokyo hotel bathroom

DO NOT ENTER.

PLEASE COME IN.

Signs on a door at a motel in America

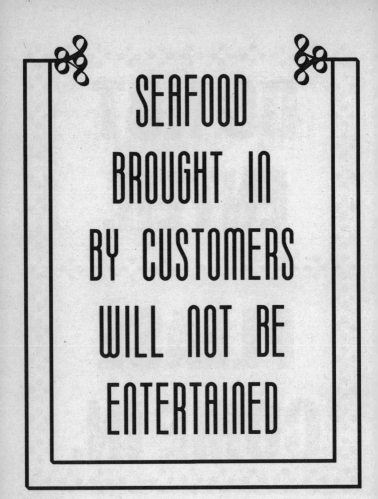

SEAFOOD BROUGHT IN BY CUSTOMERS WILL NOT BE ENTERTAINED

Sign at a restaurant in Malaysia

NON-SMOKING FORBIDDEN

Sign in hotel lobby, Jordan

IT IS
ADVISORY
TO BE
TWO
PEOPLE
DURING
ASSEMBLY

Instructions included with a
Swedish flat-packed cabinet

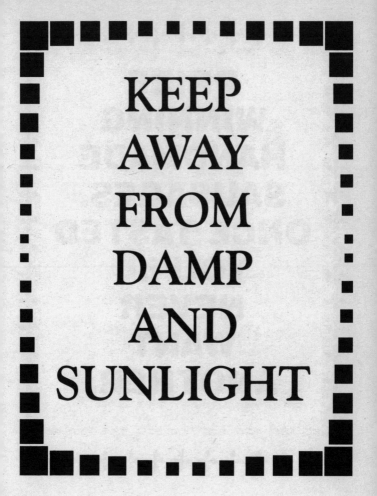

KEEP AWAY FROM DAMP AND SUNLIGHT

On a set of garden furniture

PRIZE WINNING HANDMADE SAUSAGES. ONCE TASTED YOU'LL NEVER WANT ANOTHER.

Sign at a farm shop

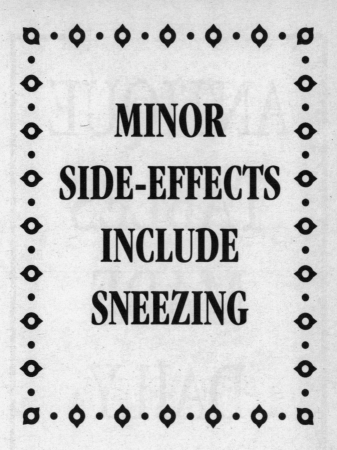

MINOR SIDE-EFFECTS INCLUDE SNEEZING

**Safety warning on
hay fever nasal-spray remedy**

ANTIQUE
TABLES
MADE
DAILY

Sign by a roadside in America

WARNING:
DO NOT DRIVE WHILST USING THIS PRODUCT

On a packet of condoms

JESUS IS COMING!

NO BINGO ON SUNDAY

Notice outside a US church

CAUTION:
WATER ON
ROAD
DURING RAIN

American road sign

FOR BEST RESULTS, START WITH CLEAN BATHTUB BEFORE USE

On a bottle of bathtub cleaner

DIETING GROUP WILL MEET AT 7PM AT THE FIRST PRESBYTERIAN CHURCH.

PLEASE USE LARGE DOUBLE DOOR AT THE SIDE ENTRANCE.

Notice on a church bulletin board

IF YOU GET THIS LIQUID IN YOUR EYE RINSE CAREFULLY WITH WATER

Instructions on a bottle of distilled water in a research laboratory

ANY MEMBER
OF STAFF WHO
NEEDS TO TAKE
THE DAY OFF
TO GO TO
A FUNERAL
MUST WARN THE
FOREMAN ON
THE MORNING
OF THE MATCH

Seen in a factory

TASTES SO GOOD THIS BOX NEVER CLOSES! TO CLOSE: PLACE TAB HERE

Advertising and instructions on an American cereal packet

Notice on Norfolk village shop door

PLEASE MIND THE STEPS

Outside a dancing academy

TODAY'S
SPECIAL
POT OF TEA
WITH STONES
AND JAM

Sign in a tea shop

Notice in hairdresser's window

OPEN
24 HOURS
EXCEPT
2AM-8AM

Sign in London pizza parlour

BABY SHOW

ALL ENTRIES TO BE HANDED IN AT THE GATE

Sign at a garden fête

WAITRESSES REQUIRED FOR BREAKFAST

In a café window

NO CHILDREN ALOUD

Outside a very exclusive boutique

CUSTOMERS WHO FIND OUR WAITING STAFF RUDE SHOULD SEE THE MANAGER

In a restaurant

IF YOU ARE SATISFACTORY PLEASE TELL YOUR FRIENDS IF YOU ARE NOT SATISFACTORY PLEASE TELL THE WAITER

In a Chinese restaurant

TRY OUR LOCAL BUTTER NOBODY CAN TOUCH IT

In a grocery shop

OUR MOTTO: WE PROMISE YOU THE LOWEST PRICES AND WORKMANSHIP

Outside a furniture shop

AUTO
REPAIR
SERVICE.
FREE PICK-UP
AND DELIVERY.
TRY US ONCE,
YOU'LL NEVER
GO ANYWHERE
AGAIN.

Outside a garage

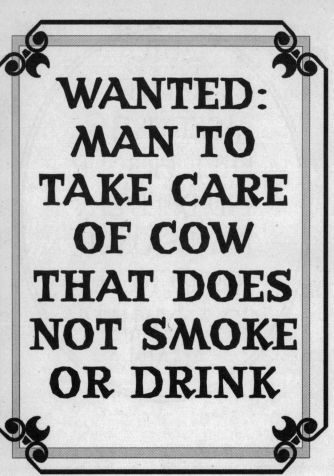

WANTED: MAN TO TAKE CARE OF COW THAT DOES NOT SMOKE OR DRINK

Sign on a farm

OUR BIKINIS ARE EXCITING. THEY ARE SIMPLY THE TOPS.

Advert in a dress shop window

SEWERS WANTED

Sign in a dry cleaner's

FOR RENT

SIX ROOM

HATED

APARTMENT

Advert in local shop window

Now you can order superb titles directly from **Michael O'Mara Books**.

The One Hundred Stupidest Things Ever Done	Ross & Kathryn Petras	£3.99
The Stupidest Things Ever Said	Ross & Kathryn Petras	£3.99
Stupid Movie Lines	Ross & Kathryn Petras	£3.99
Stupid Sex	Ross & Kathryn Petras	£3.99
Stupid Things Men Do		£3.99
The World's Stupidest Laws	David Crombie	£3.99
Strange Tails	Kohut & Sweet	£4.99
The Little Book of Farting	Alec Bromcie	£1.99
The Complete Book of Farting	Alec Bromcie	£4.99

Please allow for postage and packing:
UK: free delivery.   Europe: add 20% of retail price.
Rest of World: add 30% of retail price.

To order any of the above or any other Michael O'Mara titles, please call our credit card orderline or fill in this coupon and send/fax to:

Michael O'Mara Books, 250 Western Avenue, London W3 6EE, UK

Telephone 020 8324 5652 Facsimile 020 8324 5678

I enclose a UK bank cheque
made payable to MOM Bookshop Ltd for £_____

Please charge £_____ to my Access/Visa/Delta/Switch

Card No:_____

Expiry date:_____Switch Issue No._____

NAME (Block Letters please):
_____

ADDRESS:
_____
_____

POSTCODE: _____TELEPHONE:_____

SIGNATURE: _____